Janie Donaldson

Add-a-Line

EXTREME

QUILTING
Patterns

Dedication

To Mom, forever and with love. Thank you for teaching me how to sew and make patterns.

To my children, who inspire me to grow with new technologies and to stay young and up-to-date.

To my husband, David, for his patience and for encouraging me to rely on God, keeping the focus on all good things.

To my dream sisters, who encourage me to be creative. Thank you for all your support and your positive input.

To Helen Squire, my editor and advisor, whom I so admire.

To Valerie Cook, my friend and piecing partner.

Detail from THE HEART OF AN ANGEL, by the author

Located in Paducah, Kentucky, the American Quilter's Society (AQS) is dedicated to promoting the accomplishments of today's quilters. Through its publications and events, AQS strives to honor today's quiltmakers and their work and to inspire future creativity and innovation in quiltmaking.

Editor: Helen Squire
Graphic Design: Lynda Smith
Cover Design: Michael Buckingham
Photography: Charles R. Lynch

Library of Congress Cataloging-in-Publication Data

Donaldson, Janie.
Add-a-line : extreme quilting patterns / By Janie Donaldson.
p. cm.
Summary: "A pattern book containing continuous line patterns. Patterns are color-coded and can be used by professional and home quilters. You can use these patterns on longarm or domestic sewing machines"--Provided by publisher.
ISBN 978-1-57432-945-2
1. Patchwork--Patterns. I. Title.

TT835.D664 2007
746.46'041--dc22

2007028930

Additional copies of this book may be ordered from the American Quilter's Society, PO Box 3290, Paducah, KY 42002-3290, or online at: www.AmericanQuilter.com.

THE HEART OF AN ANGEL, 72" x 72", by the author

Contents

One for the Money – Single-Line Quilting

Two for the Show – Double-Line Quilting

Add-A-Line **Extreme** Quilting Patterns • *Janie Donaldson*

Contents

Three to Get Ready – Triple-Line Quilting

Four to Go – Quadruple-Line Quilting

Oranges & Diamonds, page 88

Introduction

This book shows you how to take simple, continuous-line quilting designs and create complex-looking patterns through repetition. Marvelous secondary and subpatterns are created as second and third rows are quilted in! These designs were created in my own studio, so I know they work.

The five chapters progress from one-line designs to four-line designs. Multiline patterns are colorized to help you see the quilting path to follow. The last chapter shows you how the secondary patterns are formed and illustrates different configurations for setting in the rows. When choosing a pattern from the multiline designs, you can eliminate a line or two or three for a totally different look! There's a good example on page 73.

I encourage you to duplicate the patterns in any size to fit your particular quilt and give my written permission for you to do so. Rolled pantographs for the designs are available at http://www.quilt-centraltv.com.

I realize that many longarm and digitizing professionals would like to use these patterns for their own businesses. You may use these patterns freely, but cannot reproduce the book as a whole for resale. You may only digitize the designs for your personal use.

As you use these patterns, please send me photos of your finished projects. I would be extremely pleased to see your quilted creations.

Janie Donaldson

ONE FOR THE MONEY – *Single-Line Quilting*

Feather Wave

Add-A-Line **Extreme** Quilting Patterns • *Janie Donaldson*

Feather Wave

Breezy Fall Leaves

Breezy Fall Leaves

Breezy Fall Leaves Block

Genesis

Genesis

Genesis

Pond Lily

Pond Lily

Add-A-Line **Extreme** Quilting Patterns • *Janie Donaldson*

His & Her Honesty

His & Her Honesty

Pineapple

Add-A-Line **Extreme** Quilting Patterns • *Janie Donaldson*

Pineapple

Teacups

Teacups

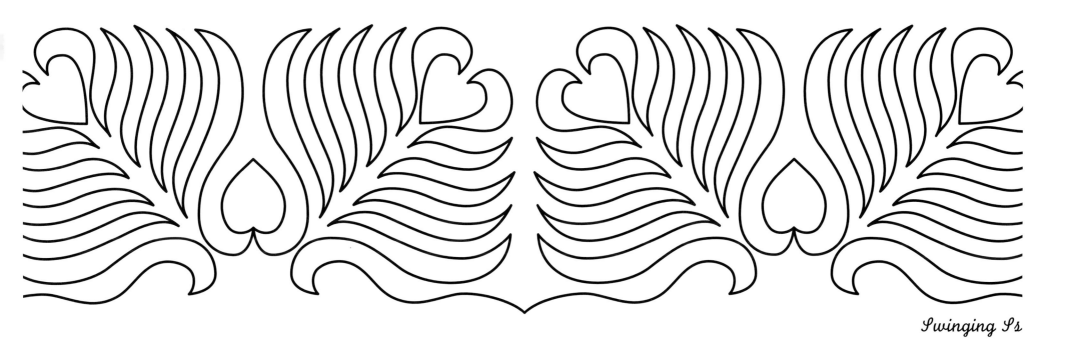

Swinging Ss

Swinging Ss

Swinging Ss Block

Leafy Inspiration – Large

Leafy Inspiration – Small

Leafy Inspiration

Sabrina's Feather Swirl

Add-A-Line **Extreme** Quilting Patterns • *Janie Donaldson*

Sabrina's Feather Swirl

Sabrina's Feather Swirl

Dewdrops on the Daisy

Dewdrops on the Daisy

Add-A-Line **Extreme** Quilting Patterns • *Janie Donaldson*

Dewdrops on the Daisy

Feathers & Pearls

Feathers & Pearls

Angel One

Angel Two

Angel One

Pinwheel Feathers

Pinwheel Feathers

Cornucopia

Cornucopia

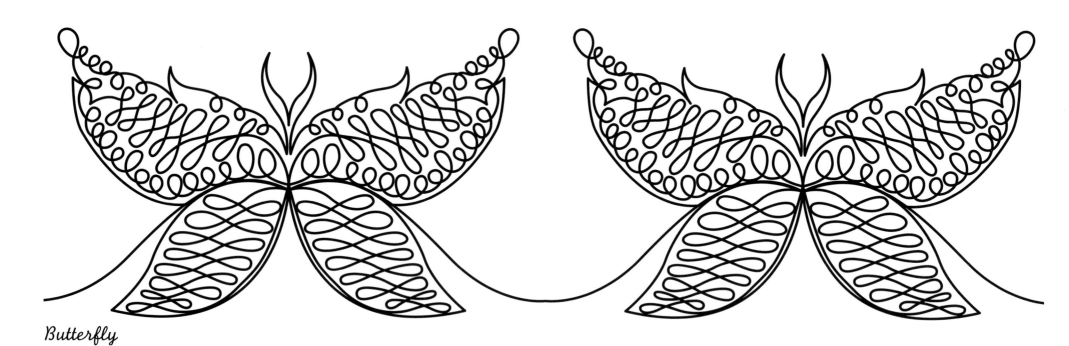

Butterfly

Add-A-Line **Extreme** Quilting Patterns • *Janie Donaldson*

Butterfly

TWO FOR THE SHOW – Double-Line Quilting

Running Horses

Running Horses

Cherokee Feathers

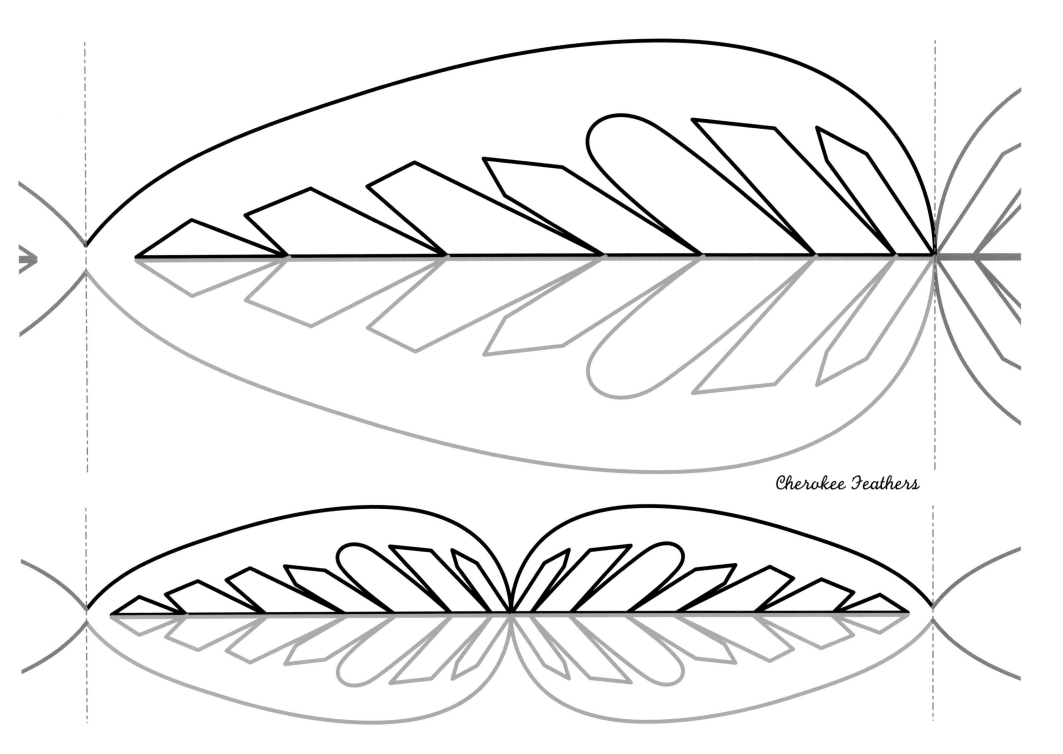

Cherokee Feathers

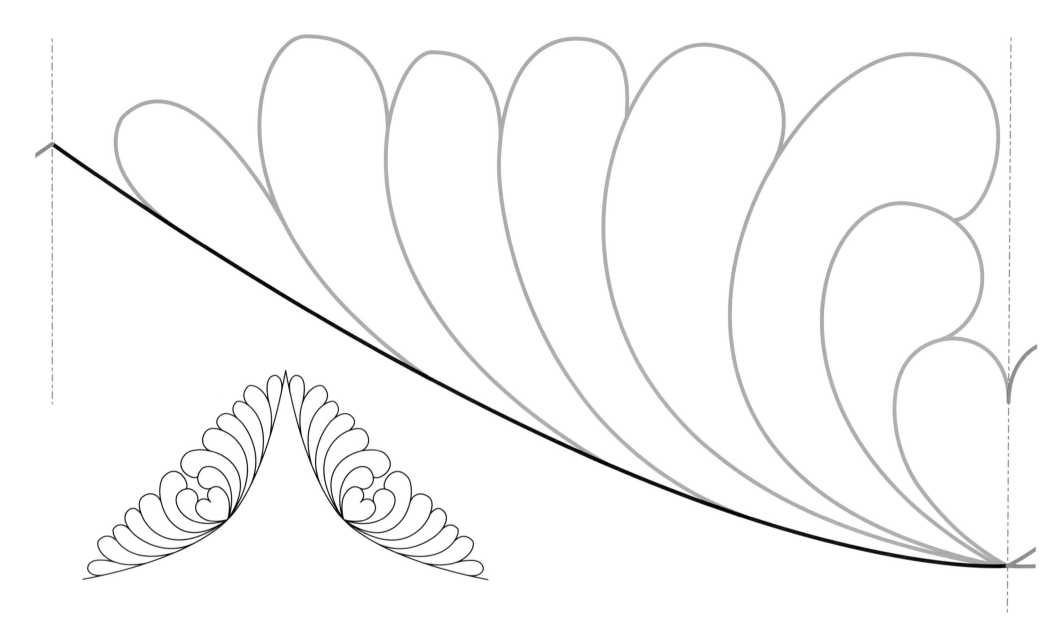

Hearts & Feathers

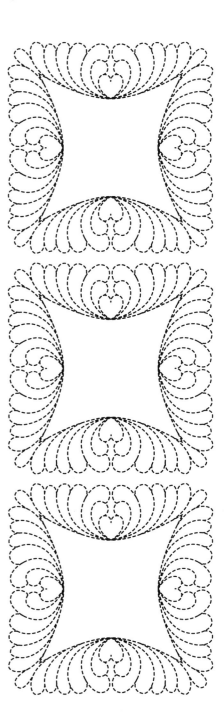

Hearts & Feathers Block

Hearts & Feathers

Feathered Diamonds

Feathered Diamonds

Classy Celtic Creation

Classy Celtic Creation

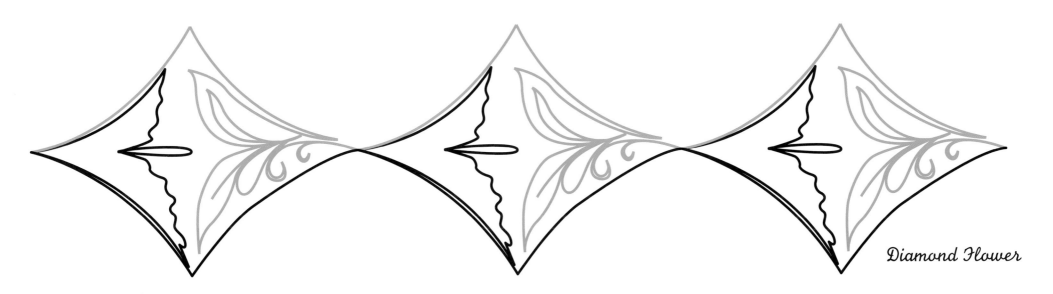

Diamond Flower

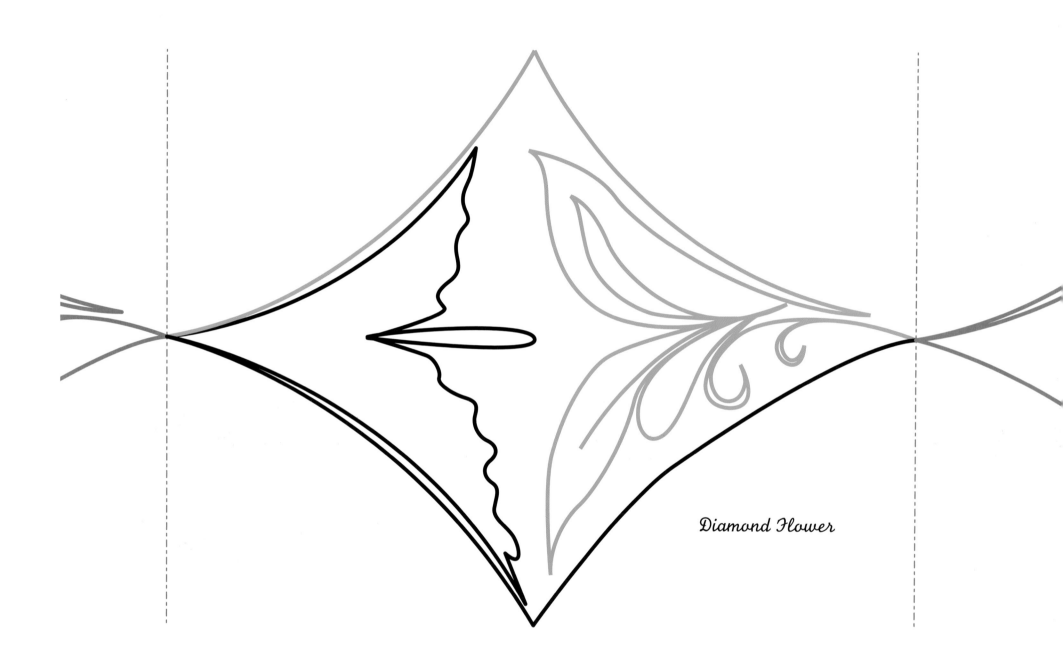

Diamond Flower

Diamond Flower

Feather Leaf

Feather Leaf

Feather Leaf Corner

Feather Leaf

Pearls & Hearts

Pearls & Hearts

Pearls & Hearts

Tu-Da-Li-Do Trumpet

Tu-Da-Li-Do Trumpet

Wild Rose Vine Repeat

Wild Rose Vine

Grapes & Leaves

Grapes & Leaves Repeat

Christmas Spice

Christmas Spice

Leafy Star

Leafy Star

Stars & Stripes

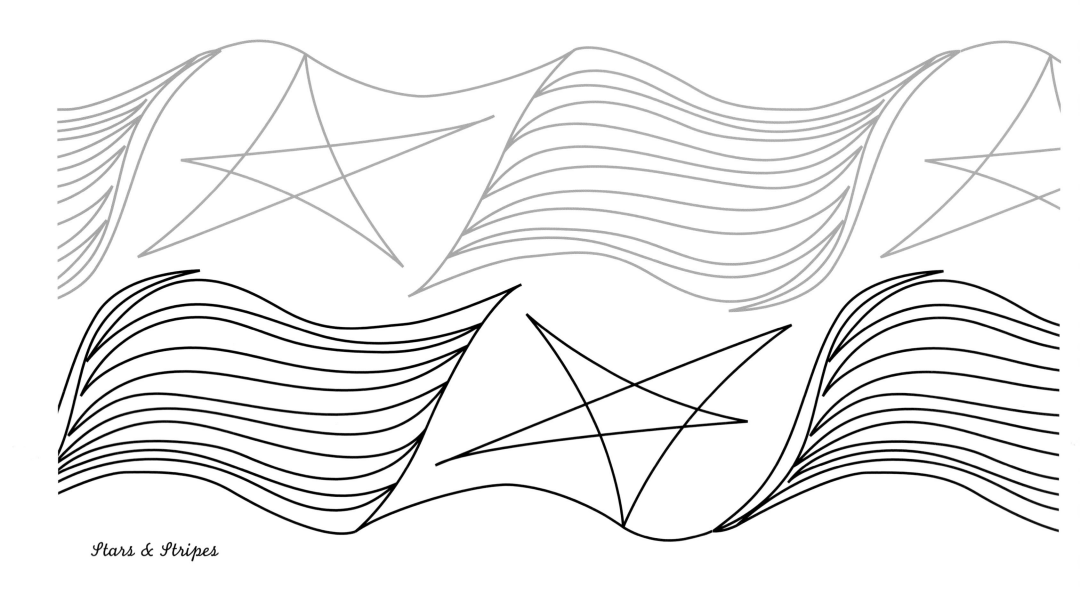

Stars & Stripes

THREE TO GET READY – Triple-Line Quilting

My Complicated Heart

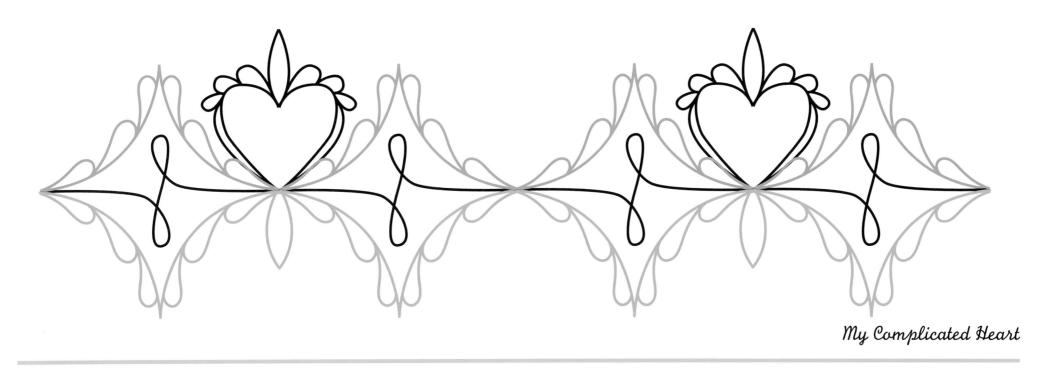

My Complicated Heart

Floral Tile

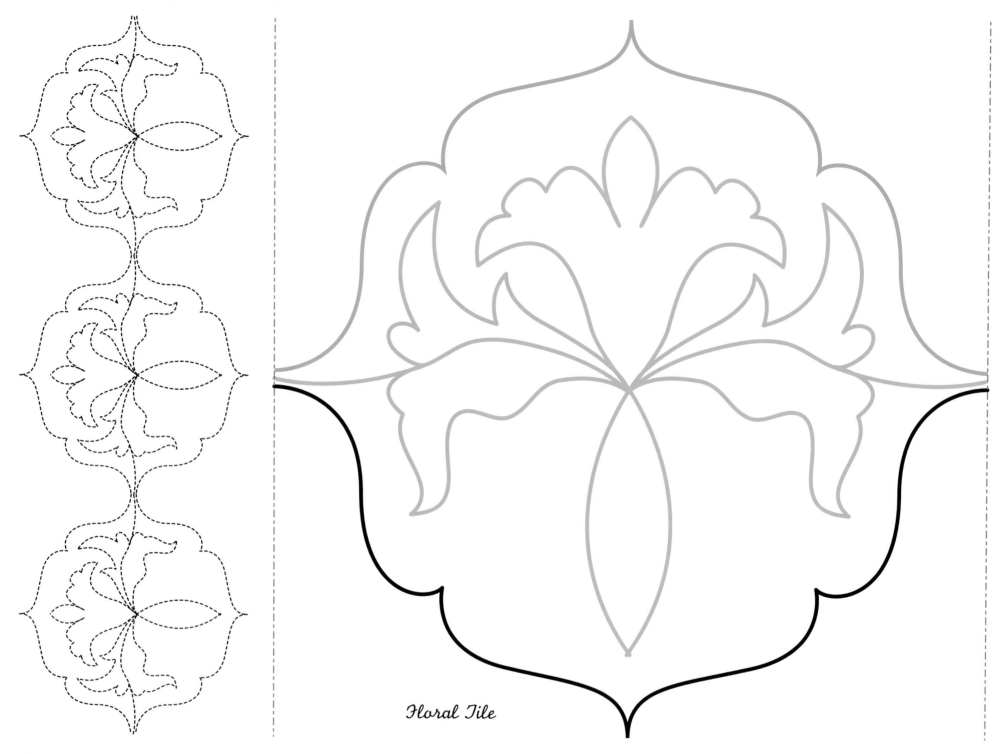

Floral Tile

Add-A-Line **Extreme** Quilting Patterns • *Janie Donaldson*

Bermuda Poinsettias

Bermuda Poinsettias

Tsunami

Add-A-Line **Extreme** Quilting Patterns • *Janie Donaldson*

Tsunami

Harps & Scrolls

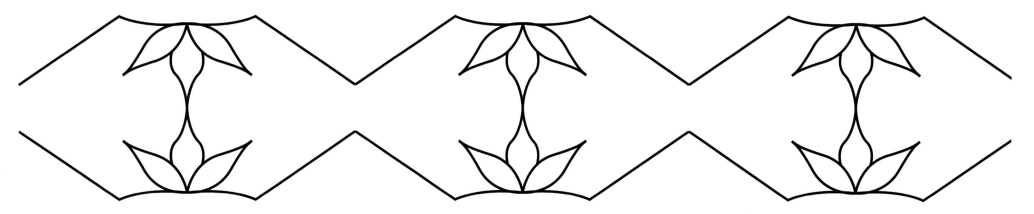

This versatile design is made from using only one of the lines from the Harps & Scrolls pattern on page 72. A great benefit of using multiline designs is that you can mix and match the lines to create something entirely new. Imagine this pattern quilted in a variegated thread. Or try quilting black fabric over a brightly colored print, which would allow you to cut away the flower areas after quilting to make a reverse appliqué piece. Another idea would be to use photos in the diamond area and then quilt between the pictures. What a quick way to create a family photo quilt!

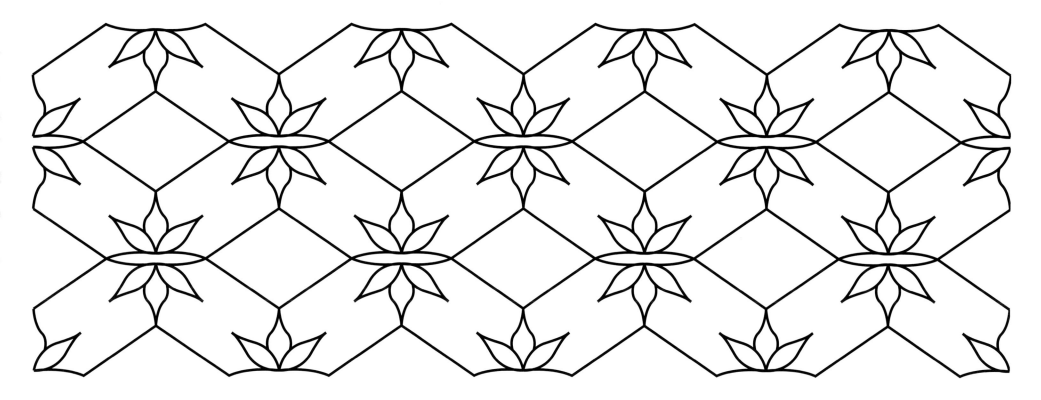

Nosegays & Scrolls

Nosegays & Scrolls

Feathered Pulpit

Feathered Pulpit

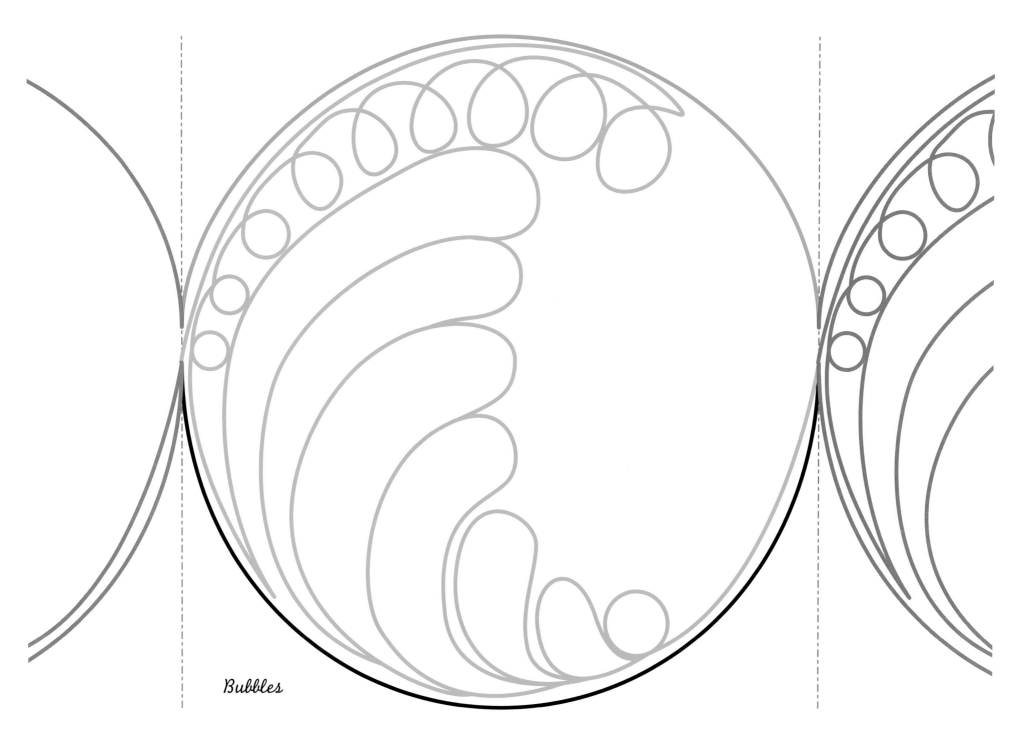

Bubbles

Modern Dutch Daisy

Daisy Mosaic

FOUR TO GO – *Quadruple-Line Quilting*

Star Blocks

Star Blocks

Tire Tread

Tire Tread

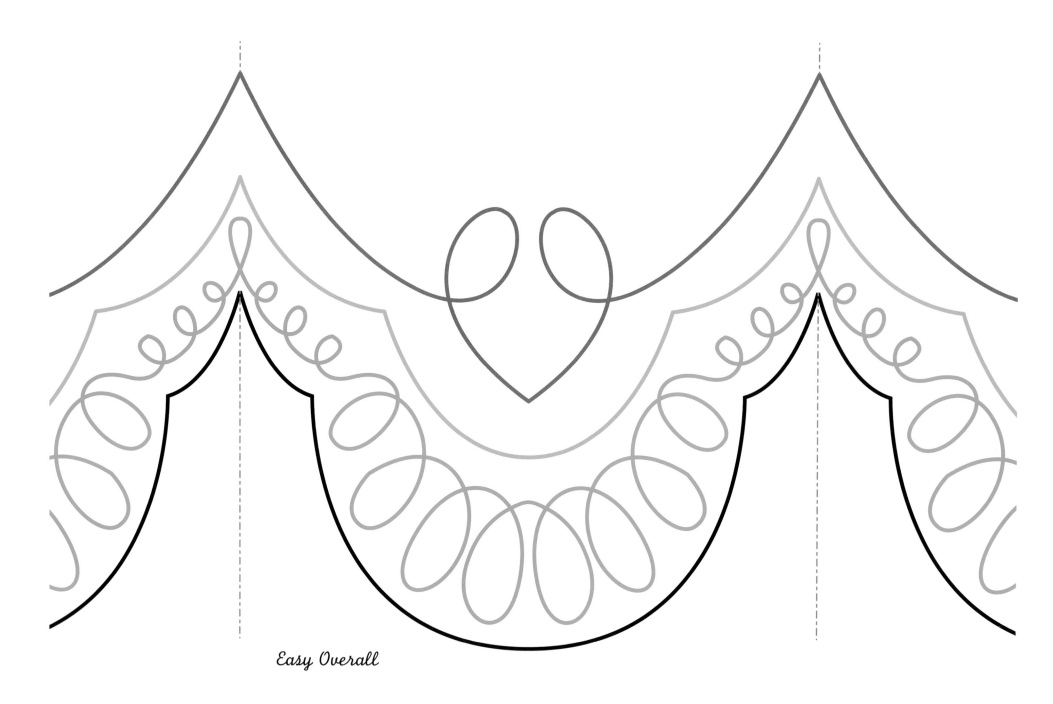

Easy Overall

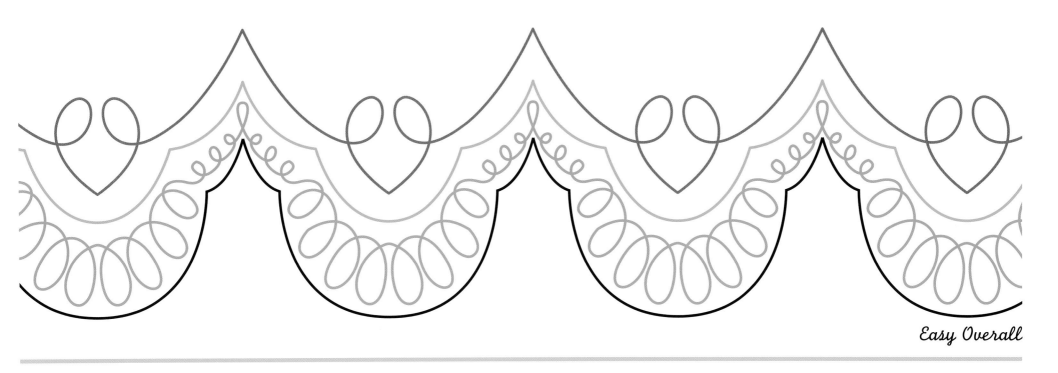

Easy Overall

Cross My Heart

Cross My Heart

Add-A-Line **Extreme** Quilting Patterns • *Janie Donaldson*

The design CROSS MY HEART from page 86 might look difficult, but it is not. Quilt in the diamond pattern first using the black and green lines, which will give you a base line and stabilize the fabric. Add the feathers and scrolls next, coming back to the base line as you proceed to the next shape. The unexpected complexity of this design may even inspire you to use it as a wholecloth quilting pattern. With your sewing or quilting machine you could also fill in the hearts with your favorite color thread to give it an embroidered, embellished look.

Cross My Heart

Oranges & Diamonds

Oranges & Diamonds

Palm Trees

Palm Trees

Janie's Favorite

Janie's Favorite

Boston Cream Pie

Boston Cream Pie

Flower Cameo

Flower Cameo

Seaweed

Seaweed

Placement Styles & Secondary Designs

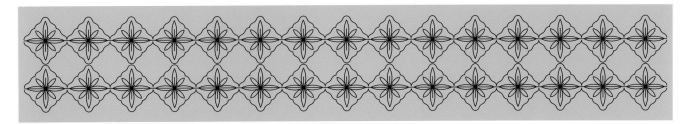

STACKED – repeated identically beneath or above each other

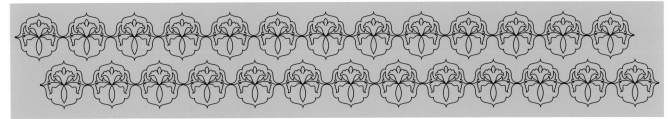

OFFSET – slid past the center point on every other row

INTERLOCKING – set into one another; interwoven

REVERSED – mirrored or placed opposite one another; can be flipped or flopped

Instead of **stacking** rows of quilting designs in identical repeats, try something new. Create additional patterns by offsetting, interlocking, or reverse and mirror imaging the rows of quilting motifs.

To **offset** rows, place a mark or piece of tape on the center of your first row and mark where the center of the next row will be positioned. If your machine is equipped with a pointer or laser light, it is a simple task to move the laser light, alternating the center marks each time and never moving the paper pattern.

To **interlock** designs, set the second pattern row a little deeper into the pre-existing pattern row. Cut a small piece of paper to use as a spacer once you decide just how closely you want the two rows positioned. Remember to measure from the same place on the design each time.

A **reversed** or **mirrored** image is simple also. It just takes a little prep time to get the pattern ready. Use one long row of the printed design and a light box to trace the reversed or mirrored design on the opposite side of the paper, right over the top of the original printing. The patterns will match and miter perfectly and the results are worth the tracing time.

Style: Stacked

Pattern: Classy Celtic Creation

Page: 46–47

Style: Stacked

Pattern: Bubbles

Page: 77

Style: Stacked

Pattern: Feathered Diamonds

Page: 44–45

Style: Reversed

Pattern: Seaweed

Page: 95–96

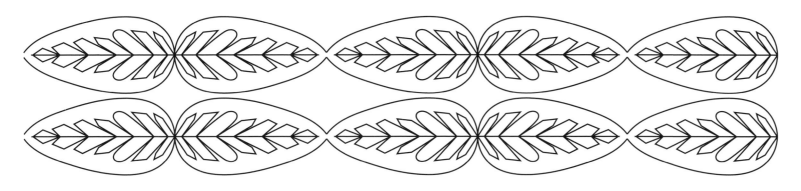

Style: Stacked

Pattern: Cherokee Feathers

Page: 40–41

Style: Reveresed

Pattern: Swinging Ss

Page: 19–21

Style: Offset

Pattern: Sabrina's Feather Swirl

Page: 24–26

Style: Reversed

Pattern: Teacups

Page: 18–19

Style: Offset & Interlocking

Pattern: Dewdrops on the Daisy

Page: 27–29

Style: Offset

Pattern: Feathers & Pearls

Page: 29–30

Style: Stacked & Allover

Pattern: Cross My Heart

Page: 85–87

Style: Reversed & Interlocking

Pattern: Leafy Inspiration

Page: 22–24

Style: Stacked

Pattern: Pinwheel Feathers

Page: 33–34

Style: Stacked

Pattern: Floral Tile

Page: 67–68

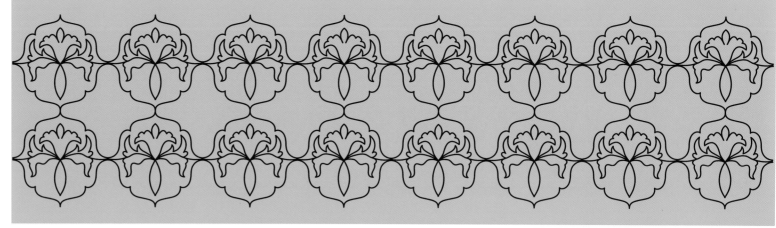

Style: Reversed

Pattern: Butterfly

Page: 36–37

Style: Stacked

Pattern: Bermuda Poinsettias

Page: 69–70

Style: Stacked

Pattern: Palm Trees

Page: 89–90

Style: Stacked

Pattern: Diamond Flower

Page: 47–49

Style: Reversed & Stacked

Pattern: Angel One

Page: 31

Style: Reversed

Pattern: Modern Dutch Daisy

Page: 75–76

Style: Reversed

Pattern: Feathered Pulpit

Page: 75–76

Style: Offset

Pattern: Cornucopia

Page: 35–36

Style: Stacked

Pattern: My Complicated Heart

Page: 66–67

Style: Stacked

Pattern: Harps & Scrolls

Page: 72

Style: Stacked & Allover

Pattern: Janie's Favorite

Page: 91–92

Style: Stacked

Pattern: Nosegays & Scrolls

Page: 74–75

Style: Reversed & Allover

Pattern: Tsunami

Page: 70–71

Style: Stacked

Pattern: Christmas Spice

Page: 60–61

Style: Reversed & Allover

Pattern: Wild Rose Vine

Page: 57–58

Style: Reversed & Stacked

Pattern: Easy Overall

Page: 84–85

Style: Reversed & Offset

Pattern: Tu-Da-Li-Do Trumpet

Page: 56–57

Style: Stacked & Allover

Pattern: Leafy Star

Page: 62–63

Style: Reversed &
Stacked

Pattern: Boston
Cream Pie

Page: 92–93

Style: Stacked

Pattern: Tire Tread

Page: 82–83

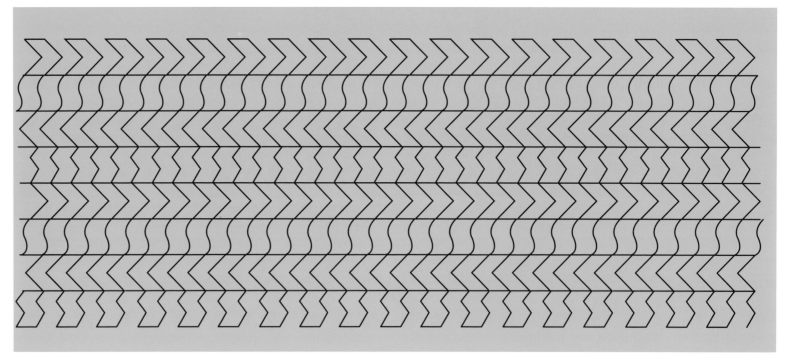

About the Author

Celebrity quilter Janie Donaldson has a strong passion for quilting, with nearly 30 years in the longarm quilting industry. Inspiration for her patterns comes from her travels in Spain, and her creativity springs from an admiration of her mother's abilities in fashion design.

Janie has grown from traditional quilting into the more innovative style of continuous-line pattern designing. Since starting Quilt Central TV in the year 2000, Janie's quilt-making has encompassed more aspects of quiltmaking than ever before. Working to develop content for over 100 episodes has given her new insights into the extreme world of quilting.

Today you will find Janie in southern Wisconsin, quilting competition pieces, gallery art, and samples for her show, Quilt Central TV. The mother of seven and a grandmother of five, her life is filled with new reasons to be inspried. Traveling and teaching are still an important part of her life with emphasis on show-and-tell lectures. Her tagline from the television show still rings true of her life: "Celebrating Quilting in Everyday Living!"

Other AQS Books

This is only a small selection of the books available from the American Quilter's Society. AQS books are known worldwide for timely topics, clear writing, beautiful color photos, and accurate illustrations and patterns. The following books are available from your local bookseller, quilt shop, or public library.

#6419 $24.95

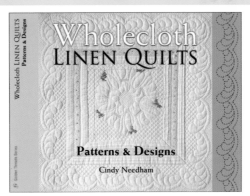

#7485 $24.95

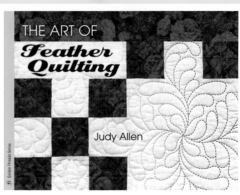

#6678 $22.95

#6069 $24.95

#7015 $22.95

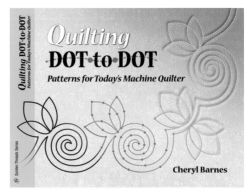

#6900 $24.95

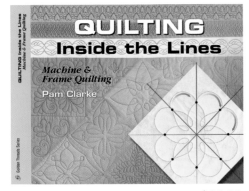

#7072 $24.95

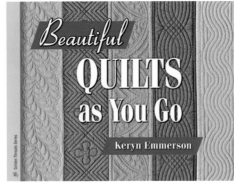

#6803 $22.95

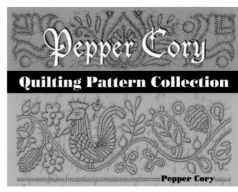

#7077 $24.95

LOOK for these books nationally.

CALL 1-800-626-5420

or **VISIT** our Web site at

WWW.AMERICANQUILTER.COM